Deism In American Thought

Woodbridge Riley

Kessinger Publishing's Rare Reprints

Thousands of Scarce and Hard-to-Find Books on These and other Subjects!

- Americana
- Ancient Mysteries
- Animals
- Anthropology
- Architecture
- Arts
- Astrology
- Bibliographies
- Biographies & Memoirs
- Body, Mind & Spirit
- Business & Investing
- Children & Young Adult
- Collectibles
- Comparative Religions
- Crafts & Hobbies
- Earth Sciences
- Education
- Ephemera
- Fiction
- Folklore
- Geography
- Health & Diet
- History
- Hobbies & Leisure
- Humor
- Illustrated Books
- Language & Culture
- Law
- Life Sciences

- Literature
- Medicine & Pharmacy
- Metaphysical
- Music
- Mystery & Crime
- Mythology
- Natural History
- Outdoor & Nature
- Philosophy
- Poetry
- Political Science
- Science
- Psychiatry & Psychology
- Reference
- Religion & Spiritualism
- Rhetoric
- Sacred Books
- Science Fiction
- Science & Technology
- Self-Help
- Social Sciences
- Symbolism
- Theatre & Drama
- Theology
- Travel & Explorations
- War & Military
- Women
- Yoga
- *Plus Much More!*

We kindly invite you to view our catalog list at:
http://www.kessinger.net

CHAPTER III

DEISM

1. The English Influences

In deism as a movement toward free-thought we have a typical example of English influence upon the American mind. It was a case of make haste slowly, for it was only by gradual degrees that British subjects emerged from the apologetic to the constructive, and from the constructive to the destructive type of free-thinking. The term free-thinker, as it first appeared in English philosophical literature, meant simply one whose thought is freed from the trammels of authority, who sought a characteristic Anglo-Saxon compromise between the Bible and the church on one side, and reason on the other. This was reflected in such works as *Christianity Not Mysterious* and *Christianity as Old as the Creation.*

Such an attitude was too vague, too apologetic. So it was succeeded by one more positive, more constructive. This attitude was reflected in a search for a natural or universal religion, a platform of belief on which all good men could unite. Such were the so-called five points common to all religions, which began with the existence of a Supreme Being and ended with future rewards and punishments. But constructive deism was, in turn, succeeded by destructive. This began when natural religion was made to supplant revealed, when prophecies were eliminated, when miracles were considered not as props

54

to belief but as mere myths. These three phases of
English deism were exhibited in the colonies. The
apologetic is represented by Cotton Mather in his
*Christian Philosopher, or A Collection of the Best
Discoveries in Nature With Religious Improvements.*
The moderate is represented by Benjamin Franklin,
who, with judicious vagueness, offered as his creed those
old points common to all religions. The destructive is
represented by Thomas Paine, who, in his *Age of
Reason,* argues boldly against mystery and miracle.
Deism, according to him, declares to intelligent man the
existence of one Perfect God, Creator and Preserver
of the Universe; that the laws by which he governs the
world are like himself immutable; and that violation of
these laws, or miraculous interference in the movements
of nature must be necessarily excluded from the grand
system of universal existence.

American deism began in a reaction against Puritan
determinism. The belief in a deity separate from the
world, an idle spectator, an absentee landlord, was a
logical rebound from the belief in a deity constantly
interfering with the world, a magical intervener, a
local busybody. Thomas Paine's *Age of Reason,* with
its notion of a creator whose "arm wound up the
vast machine" and then left it to run by itself, formed
a kind of counterpoise to Cotton Mather's *Magnalia
Christi Americana,* with its faithful record of many
illustrious, wonderful providences, both of mercies and
judgments, on divers persons in New England. In a
way, also, these two books marked the transition between
two different political points of view, one standing for
class favoritism, the other for the natural rights of
man. The Calvinistic doctrines of sovereign grace and
an elect people savored too much of the claims of British

supremacy to be long acceptable. Hence the five points of Calvinism became so many points of irritation. Total depravity might apply to effete monarchies, but not to the New World; absolute predestination to the land of passive obedience, but not to the land where men sought to be free.

Calvinism as a doctrine of necessity was, then, the proximate cause of deism as a doctrine of freedom. The notion of a partial and arbitrary deity prepared for the religion of humanity; the system of inscrutable decrees for a religion of reason. The change was striking. Talk about creatures infinitely sinful and abominable, wallowing like swine in the mire of their sins, brought about a reaction, and the next generation went from the extreme of Puritanic pessimism to the extreme of deistic optimism, the belief in the perfectibility of the human race. This change in sentiment is recorded in the attacks on the old divinity. When the consistent Calvinist merely filed smooth the rough edges of a cast-iron system, the forerunners of the Unitarian movement boldly threw the dead weight overboard. To speak in reproachful language of the moral virtues, comparing them to filthy rags, was held absurd; while the Calvinistic doctrine of the tendency of man's nature to sin, as implying his utter and eternal ruin and the torments of hell fire, was declared shocking to the human mind and contradictory to all the natural notions both of justice and benevolence.

These protests against determinism were characteristic of early American deism; but behind these acute personal reactions there were larger and quieter forces at work. In a word the dogmas of an unnatural religion were giving way to the principles of natural religion, and rationalism had at last a chance to assert itself. Here deism constituted the moving cause and the colonial college the vehicle in the transaction.

2. The Colonial Colleges and Free-Thought

Deism, as a form of rationalism, had been hanging on the skirts of Puritanism during the last quarter of the seventeenth century, but it was not until the eighteenth that it took to an independent growth and hastened the intellectual emancipation of New England. The old Boston Platform had recognized the light of nature, but more in the way of a forlorn negation than a hopeful affirmation. It spoke of natural reason as greatly impaired, saying that man retained no more of the light of reason than would conduce to tormenting reflections. From these timid limitations there arose the desire for a change from a gloomy theology to a cheering theodicy, from the doctrine of inscrutable decrees to the belief in rational purpose and benevolent design in the universe. This change is marked by two such representative works as Mather's *Reasonable Religion* and Chauncy's *Benevolence of the Deity*.

Cotton Mather did not attain his rationalistic results without some mental perturbation. At first his attitude was that of one opposed to the use of reason. Thus he uttered the warning: "Hearken ye of Harvard and Yale College to old Eubulus, exhorting you with his counsel. In most academies of this world nothing is acquired but worldly wisdom; the philosophy taught in them is nothing but foolosophy." After such strictures as these it is rather strange that Mather can avail himself of rational arguments. But this he does in his *Christian Philosophy*, where he quotes with approval the statement of an English writer that the divine reason

runs like a golden thread through the whole leaden mine
of brutal nature. Applying this principle to whatever
he saw about him, he exclaims:

How charming the proportion and pulchritude of the leaves,
the flowers, the fruits. How peculiar the care which the great
God of nature has taken for the safety of the seed and fruit!
When the vegetable race comes abroad, what strange methods
of nature are there to guard them from inconveniences. How
nice the provision of nature for their support in standing and
growing, that they may keep their heads above ground and
administer to our intentions; some stand by their own strength,
others are of an elastic nature, that they may dodge the violence
of the winds: a visible argument that the plastic capacities of
matter are governed by an all-wise infinite agent. Oh! the
glorious goodness of our deity in all these things!

There was a note in this little book that did not die.
While its scientific arguments for design fell flat, its
æsthetic elements lived on; it anticipated by a century
the transcendentalist's love of nature for its own sake.
Mather might have said with Emerson '' Come into the
azure and love the day.'' Belonging to the same school
of apologetic deists as Mather but of far higher rank
was Charles Chauncy. In his *Benevolence of the
Deity*, in place of a being cruel, inscrutable, acting by
particular providences, we find a being benevolent, rational, acting in harmony with wise goodness and accu-
rate justice. The deity does not communicate being
or happiness to his creatures by an immediate act of
power, but by concurring with an established course
of nature. He makes them happy by the intervention of
second causes, operating in a stated, regular, uniform
manner.

Chauncy's work combines sound matter with a noble
style; it marked a notable advance in the progress of

rationalism.   To teach that man is free and not determined; active and not passive; perfectible and not depraved, was to sum up the three great tenets of deism gained by way of painful reaction against the harsher doctrines of Calvinism.   The way in which this reaction came about may be traced more closely in the later writings of the Harvard worthies, who possessed one notable means for the public expression of their views. This was the Dudleian lectureship founded for " the proving, explaining, and proper use and improvement of the principles of natural religion."   The significance of this lectureship is that it furnishes an historical cross-section of the American mind.   In it may be observed not only the rise and progress of deism, but also its destruction through a number of powerful solvents.   The first of the Dudleian discourses furnishes an appropriate introduction to the whole course by giving an historical summary of the problems of dualism as connected with cosmology.   Here President Edward Holyoke was the initial speaker:

There were three opinions as to the existence of the world. One was that it was from Eternity, & Plato it seems, was the Father of it, and thought it flowed from God as Raies do from the Sun, where, by the way, we may note, That tho' they tho't the world to be eternal, yet that it proceeded from God; his Scholar also, Aristotle, propagated the same Notion & asserted that the world, was not generated so as to begin to be a world, which before was none.   He supposes preexistent & eternal Matter as a Principle and thence argu'd the world to be eternal. . . . Another Opinion as to the Existence of the world, was that it came into this beautiful Form, by Chance, or a fortuitous concourse & jumble of Atoms, This is by all known to be the Philosophy of Epicurus, & his Notion was, that the Universe consisted of Atoms or Corpuscles of various Forms & Weights, which having been dispers'd at Random thro' the immense Space, fortuitously concur'd, into innumerable Systems or Worlds, which were thus formed, & afterward from time to time increased, changing & dissolving again without any certain, Cause or Design, without the Intervention of any Deity, or the intention of any Providence. And yet this Philosopher did not deny the Existence of a God, but on the Contrary asserted it, but tho't it beneath the Majesty of the Deity to concern himself with humane affairs. . . . But the most prevailing *Opinion* . . . was, *That the world had a beginning,* & was form'd by some great and excellent Being whom they called God. And this indeed is a tho't that is perfectly agreeable to Reason.

The first Dudleian lecturer granted that natural religion was not unreasonable. A certain successor twenty years after argued for what he calls a coincidence of natural and revealed religion. He presents his arguments in a sort of imaginary conversation:

Reason would say: " Surely this stupendous universe is the work of some invisible agent, beyond all comparison & conception superiour to man; for such a grand complete System so infinitely complicate, & yet so exactly adjusted in all its parts, the most minute as well as the grandest, that all kinds of symmetry and perfection concur to complete the whole, could never be the effect of chance or the product of endless essays & mutations of matter. This Agent must have an unlimited mind, to comprehend these vast innumerable works in one perfect Idea, before they were made. His *power* also must be equal to his unlimited understanding. And he is evidently as *good* as he is wise and powerful; otherwise malignity against his creatures would appear in universal discords through nature, perpetually generating all manners of evil. . . . In some such manner as this Reason in its perfect state might be supposed capable of arriving at the knowledge of the *One True God,* & deducing from thence a compleat system of natural religion. Yet it can hardly be conceived, according to our experience of the labour of searching out truth, that the human mind, in its utmost strength, could by one glance of thought discover all the essential characteristics of the Deity, or the proper acts of worship & obedience which he requires. We might as well affirm, that unimpaired reason must naturally, at the first view of the heavenly bodies, have a clear knowledge of their magnitudes, distances and revolutions: or by looking round on the earth, immediately be acquainted with the innumerable gradations of animal life, & vegetable productions & fossils of all forms & kinds. . . . Therefore it may be justly questioned whether it would not have cost the labour of Ages to demonstrate a true System of religion, as it has taken nearly six thousand years to search out the laws of the material system & bring natural philosophy to its present perfection."

The arguments just presented were delivered in the year before the Declaration of Independence. It was not until after the second war with England that the Dudleian lectures show the weakening of the old conservative scheme under the assaults of the destructive deists. But it remained for a lecturer of the year before the publication of Emerson's *Nature* to recognize the drift of a priori arguments for natural religion as leading to the self-sufficiency of nature. Abstract arguments, reasons John Brazer in 1835, are objectionable because they virtually assume the point to be proved. Thus, the axiom that every effect has a cause avails little with those who deny that the universe is an effect; the axiom that whatever begins to exist must have had a cause of its existence, will have no pertinency with those who, like the ancient and modern Epicureans, assert that the universe is eternal and the creative power, whatever it be, only plastic. Again, the statement that every contrivance must have a contriver is no argument to him who denies that there is any proof of contrivance further than the particular instance in question is concerned, as did Hume. Finally, the prin-

ciple that nothing can be a cause of its own existence
will conclude little against him who asserts that the
world is an exception to this general rule,—it being self-
existent, as Spinoza maintained.

We have here at Harvard an hypothetical approach
to pantheism. In this free-thought had achieved a vic-
tory over the old dualism. Instead of a creator and
creation separated by a gap which could not be bridged,
instead of the old doctrine of transcendence with which
the apologetic deist had begun, we have now the doctrine
of immanence,—the very affirmation of Emerson that
nature, comprehending all existence, may be its own
cause.

The rise of deism in the second oldest of the New
England colleges is much like that in the first. At
Harvard deism as a movement of enlightenment de-
veloped through opposition. Cotton Mather, with his
eye upon the free-thinkers, had declared that " to question the being of God would be exalted folly." Similar
academic attempts to stem the tide of rationalism were
early made at Yale. In spite of them the freshening
currents came stealing in. At New Haven, as at New
Cambridge, the heads of the college could not escape
the eclectic spirit of the times. Rector Thomas Clap
avowed that the great design of founding this school
was to educate ministers " in our own way "; nevertheless, he based his moral philosophy on the deistic Wollaston's *Religion of Nature*. But there was another
head of the Connecticut college who more clearly showed
the pervasive influence of English thought combined
with the mental independence of a young colonial. It
was President Ezra Stiles, who nourished a hope that
America might be a land of British liberty in the most
complete sense. As student and tutor he had read

through some thirty-odd deistic works left to the college library by Bishop Berkeley. These books did much to open the eyes of their reader; at the same time they did not lead him into the most radical skepticism. He recounts how he read Clarke's *Demonstration of the Being and Attributes of God,* but did not find entire satisfaction; how he read Shaftesbury's *Characteristics* and admired them as sublime views of nature and of the moral government of the Most High. But he could not go beyond this the Deist's Bible and accept the conclusions of the arch-skeptic Hume. Against the latter's strictures upon the evidences of Christianity he exclaims, " Shall a King be able by a Seal and other infallible Signatures to evince his Proclamations to his Subjects so that they shall have no doubt of his Majesty's Will: and shall the Great Omnipotent King of the Universe be unable to evince & ascertain his Will to such a handfull of Intelligences the small System of Man? "

Having described the moral jaundice of the leader of skepticism in old England, Stiles as Anglus-Americanus turns to the movement in New England and gives a vivid account of the agitations of local thought during the French and Indian War:

. . . As we are in the midst of the struggle of Infidelity I expect no great Reformation until that [Revelation] is demonstratively established. . . . From the Conduct of the Officers of the Army you entertain an Expectation favorable to Virtue. Far from this I imagine the American Morals & Religion were never in so much danger as from our Concern with the Europeans in the present War. They put on indeed in their public Conduct the Mark of public Virtue—and the Officers endeavor to restrain the vices of the private Soldiery while on Duty. But I take it the Religion of the Army is Infidelity & Gratification of the appetites. . . . They propa-

gate in a genteel & insensible Manner the most corrupting
and debauching Principles of Behavior. It is doubted by many
Officers if in fact the Soul survives the Body—but if it does,
they ridicule the notion of moral accountableness, Rewards &
Punishments in another life. . . . I look upon it that our
Officers are in danger of being corrupted with vicious principles, & many of them I doubt not will in the End of the
War come home minute philosophers initiated in the polite
Mysteries & vitiated morals of Deism. And this will have an
unhappy Effect on a sudden to spread Deism or at least Scepti-
cism thro' these Colonies. And I make no doubt, instead of
the Controversies of Orthodoxy & Heresy, we shall soon be
called to the defence of the Gospel itself. At Home the
general grand Dispute is on the Evidences of Revelation—
some few of your small Folks indeed keep warming up the old
Pye, & crying Calvinism, Orthodoxy &c—these are your
Whitefields, Romaines, &c that make a pother: but the greater
Geniuses among the Ministers are ranging the Evidences of
Revelation to the public View, expunging the Augustine In-
terpretations of Scripture with the other Corruptions of the
Latin Chh, yet retained among protestants—and endeavoring
a just & unexceptionable, rational Explication of the great
Doctrines of the Gospel. The Bellamys &c of New England
will stand no Chance with the Corruptions of Deism which, I
take it, are spreading apace in this Country. I prophesy
your Two Witnesses will avail more towards curing the Con-
tagion than thousands of Volumes filled with cant orthodox
phrases & the unintelligible Metaphysics of Scholastic Divinity,
which is a Corruption of Christianity with *arabian* philosophy.

Yet Stiles was no such reactionary as some of his
correspondents thought. He did not hold that the
overvaluing of reason tends to promote atheism. When
he was informed that Rector Clap would not suffer
a donation of certain books from the free-thinking
colony of Rhode Island, he wrote to the rigid Rector and
made a notable appeal for unrestrained thought:

. . . Different men indeed object from different motives,
some from the Love of Orthodoxy & some from the Hatred

of it, & some from the generous Sentiments of that generous & equal Liberty for which Protestants & Dissenters have made so noble a Stand. It is true with this Liberty Error may be introduced; but turn the Tables the propagation of Truth may be extinguished. Deism has got such Head in this Age of Licentious Liberty, that it would be in vain to try to stop it by hiding the Deistical Writings: and the only Way left to conquer & demolish it, is to come forth into the open Field & Dispute this matter on even Footing—the Evidences of Revelation in my opinion are nearly as demonstrative as Newton's Principia, & these are the Weapons to be used. Deism propagates itself in America very fast, & on this Foundation, strange as it may seem, is the Chh of Engld built up in polite Life. A man may be an excellent Chhman & yet a profound Deist. While public popular Delusion is kept up by Deistical Priests, sensible Laymen despise the whole, & yet, strange Contradiction! joyn it, and entice others to joyn it also.—and they say all priests are alike, we all try to deceive Mankind, there is no Trust to be put in us. *Truth* & this alone being *our* Aim in fact, open, frank & generous we shall avoid the very appearance of Evil.

The protest of Stiles was unavailing. Measures were now taken to stop the infiltration of any form of deism. By a vote of the president and fellows, students were to be established in the principles of religion according to the Assembly's Catechism, Dr. Ames's *Medulla,* and *Cases of Conscience.* Yale was now outwardly a stronghold of orthodoxy; how it came to be called a hotbed of infidelity is a matter of later times. It was not until after the Revolutionary War that the satirist could describe undergraduate skepticism, could tell how the clockwork gentleman was made " twixt the Tailor and the Player, and Hume, and Tristram and Voltaire." All this might have been expected. Action and reaction were equal. As at Harvard opposition had brought electicism, so at Yale the policy of sup-

pression brought an explosion of free-thinking upon
the advent of the Franco-American deism of Citizen
Paine and President Jefferson.

Meanwhile it is in order to follow the fortunes of
deism outside of New England, and to see how the other
colonial colleges of the first rank were laid open to the
advances of rationalism.

The first head of King's College, New York, destined
to become the future Columbia University, was that
Samuel Johnson who had been forced out of Yale because of his liberal tendencies, which were early shown
even in the reputed land of the blue laws. The very
title of his most juvenile work, *Raphael, or the Genius of
English America,* was a protest against colonial con-
servatism. But Johnson's actions spoke louder than his
words. As an undergraduate he was warned against
reading Descartes, Locke, and Newton; becoming a tutor,
he introduced these works into the college library. As a
theological student he was cautioned against a certain
new philosophy, that of Berkeley, which was attracting
attention in England, being told that it would corrupt
the pure religion of the country and bring in another
system of divinity. The warning was ineffective, for
Johnson became a clergyman in the Church of England
and sought to spread that very philosophy against which
he had been warned. What trials met the students in
the provincial seats of learning is suggested in a recently
recovered manuscript entitled: *The Travails of the Intellect in the Mycrocosm and Macrocosm.* In this juvenile work Johnson leaves the little world of Puritan
thought and emerges into the larger world of constructive deism. His scheme has as its beginning benevolence,
and as its end evidences of cosmic design. This scheme
was conceived by the author at the age of eighteen, but,

being obliged to conceal his opinions with caution, it was not for half a generation and through an English magazine that the young American was enabled fully to express his views.

To show how judicious was the rationalism of this *Introduction to Philosophy* we may explain that the purpose of this small tract, " by a gentleman educated at Yale College," was declared to be: the setting before young gentlemen a general view of the whole system of learning in miniature, as geography exhibits a general map of the whole terraqueous globe. As in the natural so in the intellectual world, young students must have a prospect of the whole compass of their business and the general end pursued through the whole.

We may here cite the case of another graduate of Yale, at King's College, whose effusions, though light like straws, showed how the wind was blowing in the deistic direction. William Livingston, in his *Remarks upon Our Intended College,* wished to have the rules free to all, offensive to no sect. Fighting the efforts of the Episcopalians to obtain control of the institution, he was charged with deism and atheism. He thereupon retorted upon his opponents with a travesty of the Thirty-Nine Articles, whose tenor may be judged by the following:

I. I believe the Scriptures of the Old and New Testaments, without any foreign comments or human explications but my own: for which I should doubtless be honoured with Martyrdom, did I not live in a government which restrains that fiery zeal, which would reduce a man's body to ashes for the illumination of his soul. . . . XXXIX. I believe that this creed is more intelligible than that of St. Athanasius and that there will be no necessity for any to write an exposition of the Thirty-Nine Articles of my faith.

The position of King's College in colonial free-thinking was significant. It was a sort of half-way house between the extreme puritanism of the North and the extreme deism of the South. The former had made God everything: the latter made man everything. Samuel Johnson was a mediator between these two views: his first book made the happiness of mankind to be God's chief end; his last made the glory of God not inconsistent with our pursuing our own happiness.

To trace the further development of deism in the colonies, we pass over the College of New Jersey, defender of the faith, opponent of rationalism, and go on to Philadelphia and Franklin.

3. Philadelphia and Franklin

"I was scarce fifteen," narrates Benjamin Franklin, "when, after doubting by turns of several points, as I found them disputed in the different books I read, I began to doubt of Revelation itself. Some books against Deism fell into my hands; they were said to be the substance of sermons preached at Boyle's Lectures. It happened that they wrought an effect on me quite contrary to what was intended by them; for the arguments of the Deists, which were quoted to be refuted, appeared to me much stronger than the refutation; in short, I soon became a thorough Deist."

We have here the confession of the most precocious of the American skeptics. There is added to it an explanation which takes in, with characteristic inclusiveness, the two factors of heredity and environment. Franklin explains that he was a free-thinker because of a free-thinking ancestor, and a deist because of a youthful overdose of Calvinism. Thus he relates how his maternal grandfather had written some homespun verse in favor of liberty of conscience, and that his father's little collection of books consisted mostly of polemical works of divinity. Although Franklin considered that some of the dogmas of the Presbyterian persuasion, such as the eternal decrees of God, election, reprobation, appeared very unintelligible and others doubtful, yet he never doubted that deity exists; that he made the world and governed it by his providence; that the most acceptable service of God was the doing good to man; that our souls are immortal; and that all crimes will be punished, and virtue rewarded, either here or hereafter.

This creed was nothing but Herbert of Cherbury's five points common to all religions, the veritable creed of a moderate deist, and yet Franklin tells how he was obliged to leave Boston when his indiscreet disputations about religion began to make him pointed at with horror by good people as an infidel and atheist. He next recounts how, being employed in London, at the age of nineteen, in composing as printer for Wollaston's *Religion of Nature Delineated,* and some of the author's reasonings not appearing well founded, he wrote a little metaphysical piece entitled *A Dissertation on Liberty and Necessity, Pleasure and Pain.* The purport of this essay was to prove the doctrine of fate from the supposed attributes of God, reasoning in some such manner as this: That in erecting and governing the world, as he was infinitely wise, he knew what would be best; infinitely good he must be disposed, and infinitely powerful, he must be able to execute it; consequently all is right.

Franklin stated that the printing of this " wicked tract " of 1725 was an " erratum " in the book of his life. That confession was probably meant to disarm criticism. The deistic fatalism of this pamphlet was as nothing compared with the strange views set forth three years later in his *Articles of Belief and Acts of Religion*. Drawn up among the regulations of the Philadelphia Junto or club for mental improvement, this document formed a kind of shopkeeper's litany, or home-service for young mechanics. Among its parts were the First Principles, Adoration and Petition, of which the last begged that the petitioner might be preserved from atheism and infidelity; the second urged the reading of deistic authors like Ray, Blackmore, and the Archbishop of Cambray; while the first, as if in conscious opposition to the Anglican creed, taught the doctrine, not of one God without parts and passions, but of many gods endowed with human passions.

Here, then, follow Franklin's peculiar

FIRST PRINCIPLES

I believe there is one supreme, most perfect Being, Author and Father of the Gods themselves. For I believe that Man is not the most perfect Being but one, rather that as there are many Degrees of Beings his Inferiors, so there are many Degrees of Beings superior to him.

Also, when I stretch my imagination thro' and beyond our System of Planets, beyond the visible fixed Stars themselves, into that space that is every Way infinite, and conceive it fill'd with Suns like ours, each with a Chorus of Worlds forever moving round him, then this little Ball on which we move, seems, even in my narrow Imagination, to be almost Nothing, and myself less than nothing, and of no sort of Consequence.

When I think thus, I image it great Vanity in me to suppose, that the *Supremely Perfect* does in the least regard such an inconsiderable Nothing as Man. More especially, since it is impossible for me to have any positive clear idea of that which is infinite and incomprehensible, I cannot conceive otherwise than that he the *Infinite Father* expects or requires no Worship or Praise from us, but that he is even infinitely above it.

But, since there is in all Men something like a natural principle, which inclines them to DEVOTION, or the Worship of some unseen Power;

And since Men are endued with Reason superior to all other Animals, that we are in our World acquainted with;

Therefore I think it seems required of me, and my Duty as a Man to pay Divine Regards to SOMETHING.

I conceive then, that the INFINITE has created many beings or Gods, vastly superior to Man, who can better conceive his Perfections than we, and return him a more rational and glorious Praise.

As, among Men, the Praise of the Ignorant or of Children is not regarded by the ingenious Painter or Architect, who is rather honour'd and pleas'd with the approbation of Wise Men & Artists.

It may be that these created Gods are immortal; or it may be that after many Ages, they are changed, and others Supply their Places.

Howbeit, I conceive that each of these is exceeding wise and good, and very powerful; and that Each has made for himself one glorious Sun, attended with a beautiful and admirable System of Planets.

It is that particular Wise and good God, who is the author and owner of our system, that I propose for the object of my praise and adoration.

For I conceive that he has in himself some of those Passions he has planted in us, and that, since he has given us Reason whereby we are capable of observing his Wisdom in the Creation, he is not above caring for us, being pleas'd with our Praise, and offended when we slight Him, or neglect his Glory.

I conceive for many Reasons, that he is a *good Being;* and as I should be happy to have so wise, good, and powerful a Being my Friend, let me consider in what manner I shall make myself most acceptable to him.

Next to the Praise resulting from and due to his Wisdom, I believe he is pleas'd and delights in the Happiness of those

he has created; and since without Virtue Man can have no
Happiness in this World, I firmly believe he delights to see
me Virtuous, because he is pleas'd when he sees Me Happy.

And since he has created many Things, which seem purely
design'd for the Delight of Man, I believe he is not offended,
when he sees his Children solace themselves in any manner of
pleasant exercises and Innocent Delights; and I think no
Pleasure innocent that is to Man hurtful.

I *love* him therefore for his Goodness, and I adore him for
his Wisdom.

Let me then not fail to praise my God continually, for it is
his Due; and it is all I can return for his many Favours and
great Goodness to me; and let me resolve to be virtuous, that
I may be happy, that I may please Him, who is delighted to
see me happy. Amen!

Franklin's First Principles form an astonishing document; they teach a veritable polytheism in a land
monotonously monotheistic. We may postpone for a
moment the search for the precise sources of this doctrine and give a general reason for its rise. It was
Franklin's penetrating gaze that saw the essential weak-
ness of the deistic tenet of transcendence. As the God
of the deist was removed farther and farther from the
world he became less and less an object of worship. This
removal occurred in both time and space. On the one
hand the conventional date of the creation was dis-
counted; geology lengthened Genesis, and the coming
into being of the world was thrust into the dark back-
ward and abysm of time. The same thing happened in
regard to space. The deity was dogmatically placed
outside the framework of the visible universe, but as that
universe was enlarged its maker was necessarily put beyond the uttermost bounds. So by a double process the
deity became less an object of worship than a vague
first cause at an infinite remove.

Franklin's strange intermediate God was perfectly logical. More than that, his pluralism of divinities had a reputable literary source. There was the prevalent belief in a graded scale of reasoning life, as when Pope sought to discover " what varied being peoples ev'ry star." More particularly, there was the familiar scheme of Wollaston, who spoke of "the fixed stars as so many suns with their several sets of planets about them." Finally, inserted in the midst of Franklin's document, there was the " Hymn to the Creator," wherein Milton sang of " Sons of light, angels, fixed stars." But we have still more exact knowledge as to what was at the very bottom of these peculiar Articles of Belief. It is known that the original manuscript was Franklin's daily companion to the end of his life, but it seems to have escaped notice, for a full century after his birth, how far he was indebted to Plato. Nevertheless it has been shown how Franklin's writings give evidence that in his youth he fell under the spell of the ancient charmer. He tells how in his sixteenth or seventeenth year he procured the *Memorabilia*. From this he adopted the Socratic method of dispute, dropping abrupt contradiction and positive argumentation and putting on the humble inquirer and doubter. To Plato, then, we may trace the polytheism of the Philadelphian. For instance, the description, in the First Principles, of the Father of the gods themselves embodies the doctrines of the *Timæus* concerning the Father who begat the world and made the eternal gods, who formed the universe and assigned each soul to a star, who was good, and being free from jealousy, desired that all things should be as like himself as possible.

Space is lacking in which to reproduce one of Franklin's delightful dialogues in the classic style, nothing to equal which for charm and fancy had so far appeared in the colonies. Space also is lacking in which to tell about his ethical schemes: his practical pocket-book for eradicating the vices; his Society of the Free and Easy, " a sect that should be begun and spread at first among young and single men, each one of whom should exercise himself with the thirteen weeks' examination of the thirteen virtues, and only then should the existence of the Society be made a matter of public knowledge."

We pass, therefore, from Franklin as the virtuous Poor Richard to Franklin as the advocate of free-thought. Here we should distinguish between his private and his public views. The best portraits of Franklin present as their mark of authenticity a secretive smile playing about his lips. This is characteristic. It suggests that what he expressed outwardly did not always obtain within. After his early speculative " errata " he assumed a cautious attitude toward religion as a public institution. Thus he writes to an anonymous correspondent, presumably Thomas Paine, that he has read his manuscript with some attention, but that the arguments it contains against the doctrine of a particular providence strike at the foundation of all religion. He therefore gives as his opinion, that though the author's reasonings are subtle, and may prevail with some readers, yet he will not succeed so as to change the general sentiments of mankind on the subject, and the consequence of the printing of the piece will be a great deal of odium drawn upon himself, and no benefit to others. He that spits against the wind spits in his own face.

Of the same nature as this homely piece of advice was Franklin's *Information to Those Who would Re-*

move to America. Here he writes that, in the New World, religion under its various denominations is not only tolerated, but respected and practiced. Atheism is unknown there; infidelity rare and secret; so that persons may live to a great age in that country without having their piety shocked by meeting with either an atheist or an infidel. This is a jesuitical generalization, its truth being contradicted by the single fact that when Franklin made a motion for the holding of prayers in the Constitutional Convention, as a means of correcting the melancholy imperfections of the human understanding, he added in a satirical note, that the convention, except for three or four persons, held prayers to be unnecessary.

These are contradictory statements, but there was a reason why Franklin's writings and private beliefs did not hang together. The reason was his utilitarian point of view: he might consider free-thinking as a thing good in itself, but like his electric fluid, it was to be guided and conducted into safe channels. In spite of his general attitude of caution there were certain times when he took a firm stand against intellectual and religious coercion. This was shown in the aid he extended to the radical Joseph Priestley, author of the *Corruptions of Christianity;* also in his request to Cadwallader Colden to stop prosecution of the editor of the *New York Gazette,* for publishing a defense of deism; and finally in his letter to Ezra Stiles of Connecticut, wherein he reiterates the deistic creed of his youth, confesses that he believes that primitive Christianity has received corrupting changes, and concludes with the observation that he does not perceive that the Supreme takes it amiss by distinguishing the unbelievers in his government of the world with any peculiar marks of displeasure.

The result of Franklin's liberal policy was that Philadelphia in his day was in the van of intellectual progress. When John Adams sarcastically observed that the
place considered itself the pineal gland of the United
States, one might have retorted that that was true since
Franklin was the seat of its intellect. It was due to his
influence as founder that the University of Pennsylvania
became noteworthy for requiring no religious test
of its instructors, and for being so unprejudiced
as to bestow an honorary degree even upon Thomas
Paine.

Forced to be cautious at home it was in France that
Franklin came out in his true colors. On his mission to
Paris in 1776 he showed a remarkable liveliness of
spirits for a man of seventy. A kind of Socrates in small-
clothes, he preserved to the last the ancient irony, the
mastery of dialogue he had shown in his youthful essays. Upon his arrival, being publicly introduced to
Voltaire, he was hailed as the Solon embracing the
Sophocles of the age. And Condorcet made the remarkable eulogy which contains the parallel between these
two men as representatives of philosophy rescuing the
race of man from the tyrant fanaticism. What the old
diplomat was thought to believe at this time is told in
a conversation which John Adams recounts having had
with De Marbois, later secretary of the French legation
in the United States: '' All religions are tolerated in
America,'' said M. Marbois, '' and the ambassadors have
in all courts a right to a chapel in their own way; but
Mr. Franklin never had any.'' '' No,'' said I, laughing,
'' because Mr. Franklin had no——'' I was going to
say what I did not say, and will not say here. I stopped
short and laughed. '' No,'' said M. Marbois, '' Mr.
Franklin adores only great Nature, which has interested

a great many people of both sexes in his favor.''
'' Yes,'' said I, laughing, '' all the atheists, deists, and
libertines, as well as the philosophers and ladies, are in
his train,—another Voltaire, and thence——'' '' Yes,''
said M. Marbois, '' he is celebrated as the great philosopher and the great legislator of America.''

4. VIRGINIA AND JEFFERSON

As Philadelphia was intellectually dominated by Ben-
jamin Franklin, so was Virginia by Thomas Jefferson.
How firmly the latter stood for liberty of thinking is
manifest in the President's express desire to have in-
scribed on his tomb: '' Author of the Declaration of
American Independence, of the Statute of Virginia for
Religious Freedom, and the Father of the University of
Virginia.'' As the advocate of free-thought in the Old
Dominion, Jefferson was but the embodiment of his class.
In contrast to the heresy-hunting Calvinists of the North,
he typified the fox-hunting Arminians of the South. His
earliest intellectual impressions were gained from that
local species of Anglican clergy who, from reading the
fashionable, skeptical literature of the mother country,
came to be considered as lax in thought as they were
reputed to be loose in living.

Besides the Cavalier clergy, the College of William
and Mary had marked influence on Jefferson's mind.
In addition to the liberty of philosophizing advocated
in its charter the scientific spirit prevailed in the place.
William Small, friend of Watt, the inventor of the
steam engine, and of Erasmus Darwin, the grandfather
of the evolutionist, came to the Virginia institution in
1758, and Jefferson, who attended his lectures in natural
philosophy, declared that he fixed the destinies of his

life. Adding to these liberalizing forces the elective
system of studies, and the naturally volatile temper of
the Southerner, it was inevitable that Jefferson should
develop that receptive spirit which made him the typical
progressive of his times. As he wrote in regard to the
proposed University of Virginia: the Gothic idea that
we are to look backwards instead of forwards for the
improvement of the human mind, is not an idea which
this country will endure.

These were glittering generalities in education, but
Jefferson backed them up by specific details. For the
education of the young there was offered a scheme of
Jeffersonian simplicity,—it was to start the inquiring
student with books of a harmless sort and gradually
and insidiously to wean him away from orthodoxy. He
might begin with Hutcheson's *Moral Philosophy* and con-
tinue with Lord Kames's *Natural Religion,* but he was to
end with the *Corruptions of Christianity* by Dr. Samuel
Priestley, the Anglo-American free-thinker. It was under the influence of the latter that the great deist in
the White House, during the strenuous year of the
Louisiana Purchase, took time to write what he called
a *Syllabus of an Estimate of the Merit of the Doctrines of Jesus, compared with those of others.* In this
short work the author proposed to take first a general view of the moral doctrines of the most remarkable
of the ancient philosophers; next, a view of the deism
of the Jews, to show in what a degraded state it was;
finally, to proceed to a view of the life, character, and
doctrines of Jesus, who, sensible of the incorrectness of
their ideas of the deity and of morality, endeavored to
bring them to the principles of a pure deism.

This *Syllabus* remained a mere sketch; knowledge of
it leaked out and public charges of atheism were brought

against the President. Hence in the political agitations
of the times Jefferson declared he had had no idea of
publishing a book on religion, and that he should as
soon think of writing for the reformation of Bedlam as
the world of religious sects. So the former ambitious
project for a study of comparative religions dwindled
to a home-made harmony of the Gospels. As to the harmony, Jefferson's object was merely to take the four
Evangelists and cut out from them every text they had
recorded of the moral precepts of Jesus. There will be
found remaining, he avers, the most sublime and benevolent code of morals which has ever been offered to man.
" I have performed this operation for my own use," he
continues, " by cutting verse by verse out of the printed
book, and arranging the matter which is evidently his,
and which is as easily distinguishable as diamonds in
a dunghill. The result is an octavo of forty-six pages
of pure and unsophisticated doctrine."

This production, issued by Congress in its four-
fold polyglot form—Greek, Latin, French, English—a
full century after its inception, is the so-called Jefferson
Bible. Bearing the title *The Life and Morals of Jesus
of Nazareth,* the compiler acknowledges that it was at-
tempted too hastily, being the work of two or three
nights only at Washington, after getting through the
evening task of reading the letters and papers of the day.
To the larger undertaking Jefferson never went back,
perhaps, because he realized that the rôle of a philosophical higher critic was an impossible one, that to distinguish between primitive Christianity and later accre-
tions was a task beyond the scholar of that age. Jefferson's partial comparative studies remain as the most
formal, but not as the sole expression of his beliefs. In
addition to the *Syllabus* and the *Bible* there is a volu-

minous correspondence, from which the Virginian's somewhat motley philosophy may be reconstructed. In general, that philosophy was an eclecticism of a pronounced deistic type, since it was the very peculiarity of the deist to wear a patchwork philosopher's cloak, yet to wear it in the fashion of the day. Thus, when on different occasions Jefferson exclaimed: " I am an Epicurean," " I am a Materialist," " I am a sect by myself," there was discoverable beneath these various disguises the strut and swagger of the age of reason.

Of the different phases of thought through which Jefferson passed the most interesting was the materialistic. It was his five years' residence in France, before the outbreak of the Revolution, that gave the free-thinking Southerner an insight into the possibilities of materialism when carried to a logical outcome. As American minister Jefferson had the fortune to enjoy the society of the same lively set of spirits as did his predecessor, Franklin. Thus he could recall to Cabanis the pleasant hours he passed with him at the house of Madame Helvétius; confess that the French literati are half a dozen years ahead of the American, and yet make no effort to catch up with them.

Here Jefferson's fundamental deism held him back. Like the more moderate exponents of the Enlightenment, while disbelieving in a revealed, he was at the same time convinced of the advantages of a natural theology. So it was that " the savage from the mountains of America," living in the midst of the intellectual seductions of Paris, could still remain a believer in the Être Suprême. The system of Diderot, D'Alembert, and D'Holbach was designated by his friend, Baron Grimm, an exposition of atheism for chambermaids and barbers. Jefferson, not so witty but more wise, criticised this extreme presentation more broadly and more soberly. Remarking that the atheistic was a more numerous school in the Catholic countries, while the infidelity of the Protestant took generally the form of deism, he puts the arguments of both sides thus: When the atheist descanted on the unceasing motion and circulation of matter through the animal, vegetable, and mineral kingdoms, never resting, never annihilated, always changing form, and under all forms gifted with the power of reproduction; the theist, pointing " to the heavens above and to the earth beneath and to the waters under the earth," asked if these things did not proclaim a first cause, possessing intelligence and power.

Thus far Jefferson's view of the universe was that of a moderate deist. The same attitude is taken in his characteristic compromise between the Epicurean doctrine of the eternity of the world and the Puritanic doctrine of interference with the ordered course of nature. Calling himself a skeptical reader, he nevertheless reasons on the supposition that the earth has had a beginning. However, he does not agree with those biblical theorists who suppose that the Creator made two jobs of his creation, that he first made a chaotic lump and set it in motion and then, waiting the ages necessary to form itself, stepped in a second time to create the animals and plants which were to inhabit it.

The last phase through which the Southern thinker passed was that of natural realism, or that form of thought which emphasizes intuition and common sense. When he was young Jefferson recalls that he was fond of speculations which seemed to promise some insight into the hidden country. After his retirement from active life he rests content in the belief that there is a reality which we directly recognize in beings, and that we are guided unconsciously by the unerring hand of instinct. In defense of his final faith in the common sense of moral sense the reminiscent statesman puts this patriotic question: If our country, when pressed with wrongs at the point of the bayonet, had been governed by its heads instead of its hearts, where should we have been now? Hanging on a gallows as high as Haman's. The heads began to calculate and compare numbers; the hearts threw up a few pulsations of their warmest blood; they supplied enthusiasm against wealth and numbers; they put their existence to the hazard when the hazard seemed against us, and they saved the country.

To bring Jefferson's philosophy into bolder relief it may be compared with that of John Adams, the cautious speculator and taster of systems, who, even in the days of their political rivalry, Jefferson considered " as disinterested as the being who made him." Now, it was after their reconciliation through Benjamin Rush that the correspondence between the Whig and the Federal ex-presidents discloses two gentlemen of the old school, both omnivorous readers, both averse to Calvinism and clerical obscurantism, both interested in the rising study of comparative religion, both tinged with the current deistic thought. Of the two the Southerner was more prone to generalizations, more impatient of other men's beliefs; the Northerner more tolerant, not inclined to go beyond " New England guesses." " The Philosophical Chief of Monticello is such a heterodox and hungry fellow," so runs a doggerel couplet of the day; Adams appears equally versatile but far less ardent. Confessedly afflicted with a kind of Pyrrhonism, he numbers himself among those Protestants *qui ne croyent rien.*

Adams's ironical deprecation of his own knowledge was doubtless one reason for Jefferson's drifting away from the Gallic speculation. Adams is sensible of the services of the French philosophers to Liberty and Fraternity, yet he cannot but think that they are all destitute of common sense:

> They all seemed to think that all Christendom was convinced as they were, that all religion was "visions Judaicques" and that their effulgent lights had illuminated all the world. They had not considered the force of early education on the millions of minds who had never heard of their philosophy. And what was their philosophy? The universe was matter only, and eternal; spirit was a word without a meaning. All beings and attributes were of eternal necessity; conscience, morality, were all nothing but fate. Who, and what is fate? He must be a sensible fellow. He must be a master of science. He must calculate eclipses in his head by intuition, and what is more comfortable than all the rest, he must be good natured, for this is upon the whole a good world.

In these jocular criticisms there was a sly dig at Jefferson's deism. The French fate bore a striking resemblance to his benevolent deity, trust in whom would bring the philosophic millennium. And so Adams writes again: " Let me now ask you very seriously, my friend, where are now in 1813, the perfection and the perfectibility of human nature? Where is now the progress of the human mind? Where is the amelioration of society? . . . I leave those profound philosophers to enjoy their transporting hopes, provided always that they will not engage us in French Revolutions. . . ." And so throughout the correspondence,—the impartial Novanglian meets the strenuous Virginian with whimsical advice. When as Epicurean he becomes too stoical, he

urges him to eat his canvas-back duck; when as deist he
becomes too dogmatical, he remarks: " It has been long,
very long, a settled opinion in my mind, that there is
now, never will be, and never was but one being who
can understand the universe. And that it is not only
vain, but wicked, for insects to pretend to comprehend it."

It was easy for Adams to write in this way; an ag-
nostic's apology was tolerated in the case of one who
would leave " metaphysics in the clouds." But with
Jefferson things were different; politics complicated the
situation and faction spoiled philosophy. The Federal-
ists linked together Jeffersonianism, atheism, and the
excesses of the French Revolution. They called the
President a Jacobin, an infidel, and a republican villain.
They spoke of a dangerous, deistical, and Utopian
school of which a great personage from Virginia was
a favored pupil. They said his principles relished so
strongly of Paris, and were seasoned in such a pro-
fusion of French garlic, that he offended the whole na-
tion. In these attacks the Federal clergy of New England were implicated. When Jefferson had brought
over from France the arch-infidel Thomas Paine in a
government ship, they spoke of him as an Ephraim who
had become entangled with the heathen. Jefferson's
defenders were unable to mend matters. The author of
the *Hamiltoniad, or an Extinguisher of the Royal Faction of New England* dismisses the worn-out tale of the
President's irreligion by retorting that " he has thrown
into the lap of Morality the purest apothegms of the
Apostles and Fathers; he confounds the politicians by
calling them Tory bloodhounds, yelping upon the dan-
gers that may arise from the Virginian or Southern influence." These mixed metaphors betray a political

confusion in which Jefferson found it hard to preserve a philosophic calm. He asserted that the priests, to soothe their resentments against the act of Virginia for establishing religious freedom, wished him to be thought atheist, deist, or devil, who could advocate freedom from their religious dictations. Having opposed the scheme of a state-supported church—" Christianity for pence and power "—he pronounced Massachusetts and Connecticut the last retreat of monkish darkness and bigotry.

And so against the narrowness of the North and as a bulwark against the " pious young monks of Harvard and Yale," Jefferson proposed to erect his Southern University. In the plan for this institution which he proposed to the Virginia legislature, he intended to place the entire responsibility for religious training upon an ethical basis, where all sects could agree. As he explained the matter: " The proofs of the being of a God, the creator, preserver and supreme ruler of the universe, the author of all the relations of morality, and the laws and obligations these infer, will be within the province of the professor of Ethics; to which adding the development of these moral obligations in which all sects agree . . . a basis will be found common to all sects." Because of his plan of having no professorship of divinity and allowing independent schools of theology to be established in the neighborhood of the University, Jefferson complained that a handle had been made to disseminate an idea that this is an institution, not only of no religion, but against all religion. But in spite of his opponents' fulminations " the liberality of this State," concludes the Virginia humanist, " will support this institution and give fair play to the cultivation of reason."

5. THOMAS PAINE AND POPULAR DEISM

In examining the books of the early colleges and the
thoughts of their representative men, there have been
found numberless signs of colonial free-thinking, of
mental independency before political independence. In
addition to these academic studies there must now be
made a search for the more elusive traces of the spreading of infidelity, before the actual outburst of revolutionary thought. As has been already intimated, this
movement, beginning as a popular reaction, was more
felt than avowed, more a matter of subtle distrust than
of precise knowledge. It was the faint smoke in the
air, presaging the coming forest fire. It was a time
when the clergy might warn against " the insidious
encroachments of innovation," but when the laity pre-
ferred the Indian summer of indifference. Toleration
was pervasive. It has been described as gradually dif-
fused over the land by such fostering circumstances as
colonial impatience with prescription and custom, and
that original adventurous spirit which, combined with
dissatisfaction with home conditions and voluntary
exile, insensibly fitted the mind for the propositions of
liberty.

Of these propositions, the liberty to think and feel
as one liked was the most conducive to the coming of
free-thought. Paine's *Age of Reason* was especially op-
portune because it was in agreement with that liberty
of conscience granted or implied in so many of the Revolutionary documents. Among these documents we may
refer to Patrick Henry's Bill of Rights, in which he
held that religion can be directed only by reason. To
this Madison added that all men are equally entitled to
the full and free exercise of religion according to the

dictates of conscience. This was followed in 1785 by Jefferson's Declaratory Act, establishing religious free‐ dom in Virginia, and by the Pennsylvania constitution, advocated by Franklin, which contained the clause as to the natural and inalienable right to worship according to the dictates of the understanding. In brief, twelve out of the thirteen original States allowed an increased measure of mental freedom. It was only in Massa‐ chusetts that a dread of liberty was expressed. There we find the question debated as to whether public offices might not be held " even among those who have no other guide to the way of virtue and heaven, than the dictates of natural religion."

The political expressions of rationalism in the Revo‐ lutionary period are many, the philosophical few. Be‐ tween the Stamp Act and the adoption of the Constitu‐ tion, there was but one native work worth mentioning in the deistic connection. But Ethan Allen's *Reason the Only Oracle of Man* did not arrest the popular at‐ tention. So it remained for a naturalized American to turn the tide of thought. It was the *Age of Reason* of Thomas Paine which marked high water in the deistic movement, for it was carried upon the wave of enthusi‐ asm caused by the author's Revolutionary pamphlets *Common Sense* and the *Rights of Man*. The radical writer affirms that, as his motive in his political works had been to rescue man from tyranny and false sys‐ tems and false principles of government, so in his re‐ ligious publications it was to bring man to the right reason God had given him, unshackled by fable and the fiction of books.

The *Age of Reason* is a perfect example of the popu‐ larizing of current deistic opinions. It has the same method of so-called mathematical proof, the same me‐

chanical view of nature, the same disregard of the
problem of evil, the same aversion to mystery, the same
iridescent dream as to mankind's perfectibility, the
same delusion as to monotheism being a primitive belief,—"Adam was created a deist" says this prehis-
toric critic. In a word, the book is anything but original. With the exception of a phrase or two like the
"religion of humanity," there is not an idea in it which
cannot be matched in the writings of the English free-
thinkers of the Georgian era. Paine simply repeats, in
the language of the street, the arguments of Collins
against prophecy, of Woolston against miracles, of
Tindal against revelation, of Morgan against the Old
Testament, of Chubb against Christian morality.

This is the negative side of the book. More effective
is the positive. In place of the false "bases of Christianity" Paine would put what he calls a true theology.
He cannot see how man can hold to a system where
Satan is deified and given power equal to that of the
Almighty; where man is called an outcast, a beggar, a
mumper, calling himself a worm and the fertile earth a
dunghill, and all the blessings of life but the thankless
name of vanities. But there is a substitute for all
these corruptions "from Moloch to modern predesti-
narianism,"—it is eighteenth-century optimism, thus
grandiloquently set forth: If objects for gratitude and
admiration are our desire, do they not present themselves every hour to our eyes? Do we not see a fair
creation prepared to receive us the instant we are born
—a world furnished to our hands, that costs us nothing? Is it we that light up the sun; that pour down
the rain; and fill the earth with abundance? Whether
we sleep or wake, the vast machinery of the universe
still goes on.

The effect of the *Age of Reason* on the community may be easily imagined. The clergy attacked it, the colleges criticised it, but the populace read it. Dedicated to the author's fellow-citizens of the United States of America, it was sold for a few pence the copy or given away gratis. The first edition, printed in France, was spread broadcast through the free-thinking societies affiliated with the Jacobin Club of Philadelphia. Within two decades the pamphlet was to be found on the banks of the Genesee and Ohio; within two more it was circulated among the readers of Volney and Voltaire and in those places in Tennessee and Kentucky whose names still attest the French sympathies of the first settlers. It is astonishing how far the light of nature threw its beams. The president of Transylvania University was suspected of teaching an unrestrained naturalism, and a friend of Abraham Lincoln reported that in Indiana the *Age of Reason* passed from hand to hand, furnishing food for the evening's discussion in tavern and village store.

The book, moreover, met with that sincerest form of flattery—imitation. An example of this was Elihu Palmer's *Prospect, or View of the Moral World for the Year 1804.* According to the allegorical thunder and lightning frontispiece, the Book of Saints and Ten Commandments are being dashed to the ground from the Altar of Truth and Justice to be supplanted by the *Age of Reason* and the *Rights of Man.* Of an equally destructive aspect was George Houston's New York *Correspondent* of 1829, containing lectures delivered before the Free Press Association on the inconsistencies, absurdities, and contradictions of the Bible. This journal also presented the advanced views of Fanny Wright, a sort of Wilhelm Meister in petticoats, who wandered over the country

from Woodstock, Vermont, to Cincinnati, Ohio. The
opponents of popular deism now raised their heads.
The free-thinking societies, spread through New England and the Middle States, were designated the
banded Goths and Vandals of political atheism. The
author of the *Sceptic's Manual* retailed petty and ma-
licious gossip concerning the last days of Hobbes and
Hume, Voltaire and Paine. In the *Antidote to Deism*,
Ethan Allen is called an ignorant and profane deist,
Paine a drunkard, to reason with whom would be like
casting pearls before swine.

Such were the attacks of the minor clergy. In the
colleges the battle was waged more in accordance with
the rules of war. The most prolific of the writers against
deism, and the materialism which happened to be asso-
ciated with it, was President Timothy Dwight of Yale.
As one of the Hartford wits, he had composed a sort of
American Dunciad, the *Triumph of Infidelity*, which
was ironically dedicated to Voltaire. How that poem
confined the deist in the pillory of his own terms, and
flung into his teeth his own arguments, is to be seen
from these lines:

> "His soul not cloath'd in attributes divine;
> But a nice watch-spring to the grand machine.
>   .   .   .   .   .   .
> Enough, the Bible is by wits arraigned,
> Genteel men doubt it, smart men say it's feigned."

In contrast to this effusion were the earlier poems of
Dwight's salad days which showed a decided leaning to
the philosophy of the French Encyclopædists. In the
Columbia and the *Conquest of Canaan,* French
phrases are curiously wrought into a sort of biblical
epic on the New World. The sons of this " blissful Eden

bright '' are urged to '' teach laws to reign and save the Rights of Man.'' The author subsequently explained that these were the mock heroics of a time when the strong sympathy towards the leaders of the French Revolution prepared to make us the miserable dupes of their principles and declarations. But the doctrines of the 14th of July were not to be confused with those of the 4th of July. As the head of Yale College, Dr. Dwight became the leader of the forces against deism. His *Century Discourse* gives a trenchant account of the progress of infidelity,—its descent from the lofty philosophical discourse to the newspaper paragraph, its spread among the masses, and the ultimate return to more sober thought. '' Infidelity,'' the discourse proceeds, '' was first theism, or natural religion, then mere unbelief, then animalism, then skepticism, then partial, and finally, total atheism. The infidel writers have used terms so abstract, and a phraseology so mysterious as to attract readers fond of novelty, but the common people, never honored by Voltaire with any higher title than the rabble or the mob, have been caught by these writers, who volunteered to vindicate their wrongs and assert their rights. Happily it was soon discovered that the liberty of infidels was not the liberty of New England; that France instead of being free, merely changed through a series of tyrannies; and that man, unrestrained by law and religion, is a mere beast of prey. Even sober infidels began to be alarmed for their own peace, safety, and enjoyments.''

The air of gravity and severity about this passage is explained by what men remembered of the events following the peace of 1783, the intrigues of Genet, the terrorism incited by Freneau, when Market Street, Philadelphia, was filled with a mob, the distrust of

Napoleon implied in President Adams's proclamation. This passage is also explained by the wild and vague expectations everywhere entertained, especially among the young, of a new order of things about to commence, in which Christianity would be laid aside as obsolete. In the exultation of political emancipation, infidel philosophers found ready listeners when they represented the restraints of religion as fetters of the conscience, and moral obligations as shackles imposed by bigotry and priestcraft.

At Harvard College, the academic attitude toward deism was somewhat complicated. Federal in politics and Unitarian in religion, it was doubly averse to the enthusiasms and raptures of Franco-American rationalism; it deplored the "foul spirit of innovation," and sought some check to the "infuriated steeds of infidelity." At Princeton the *Age of Reason* was opposed by the philosophy of common sense. Where Berkeleian idealism had been driven out, the Bridgewater Treatises came in. According to its catalogue, the library abounded in volumes like *Dick's Celestial Scenery Illustrating the Perfections of the Deity,* and Prout's *Chemistry, Meteorology and the Functions of Digestion considered with reference to Natural Theology.* The favorite text-book, as in the majority of conservative colleges, was Dugald Stewart, and Stewart's aim was declared to be to stem the inundation of the skeptical, or rather atheistical publications which were imported from Europe. But a conservative literature does not alone explain the stringent policy of Princeton; behind the books were such facts as that, after the revolutionary war when the students had been "freed from all sanctuary and Sabbath restraint," there was left only a handful of students who professed themselves Christians and that, in 1802, the trustees in their " Address to the Inhabitants of the United States," declared that their purpose was to make this institution an asylum for pious youth, in this day of general and lamentable depravity.

Popular deism was rejected by the clergy and thrust out by the colleges. It remains to be seen how the public first accepted, then grew tired of it. Chancellor Kent said that in his younger days there were very few professional men who were not infidels; Ezra Ripley, that a large portion of the learning not possessed by the clergy leaned to deism. A few specific events will illustrate how this rapid growth of the army of free-thinkers was followed by an equally rapid defection from the ranks. In 1801, James Dana of Connecticut said that infidelity appeared to be gaining ground; by 1810, it was reported that infidelity abounded to an alarming degree and in various shapes in the district west of the Military Tract in New York. In 1822 an anonymous " letter to a deist in Baltimore " stated that deism is taking root rapidly and soon will grow up surprisingly and become the only fashionable religion. In Virginia about the same time Bishop Meade asserted that in every young man he met he expected to find a skeptic, if not an avowed unbeliever.

This was the advance of the movement. A reaction followed which started in protests from the church, the state, and the professions, and ended in a series of religious revivals. In 1798, the Presbyterian General Assembly uttered a warning against the abounding infidelity which tends to atheism itself; in 1800, the President referred to the dissemination of principles subversive of the foundations of all religious, moral, and social obligations, that have produced incalculable mischiefs in other countries; in 1824, Dr. Charles Caldwell thought fit to write a *Defence of the Medical Profession against the charge of Infidelity and Irreligion.* The unpopularity of deism is likewise exhibited in the light literature of the day. Fenimore Cooper describes one of his heroines as being properly impressed with the horrors of a deist's doctrines, and another as shrinking from his company. Harriet Martineau wrote back to England how she was told of one and another with an air of mystery, like that with which one is informed of any person being insane, or intemperate or insolvent, that so and so was thought to be an unbeliever.

The results of deism in America may now be briefly summed up. Among the people the majority were drawn off by an emotional substitute for thought, the revivals that swept over the country. At bottom the deistic system was too cold and formal; it externalized deity, lacked a continuing enthusiasm, and so failed to satisfy the cravings of emotional excitement. The philosophy of a Franklin might appeal to the business, it did not appeal to the bosoms of men. In the colleges those who were not affected by revivalism were held in check by circumscribed courses presenting the similarities between natural and revealed religion. Finally, among the clergy, the great part stood for orthodoxy. As expressed by one of the numerous century sermonizers, there was no neutral ground to be taken between evangelical doctrines and infidelity.

Such were the results of the hundred years' war for free-thinking,—apparently fruitless unless judged by later events. One such event was New England transcendentalism, whose programme on its negative side was almost precisely what the deists had been denying; on its positive, an assertion of what they had been lacking. Transcendentalism denied the need of miracle, revelation, dependence on an outward standard of faith; it affirmed the need of intuition, mystic ecstasy, inward dependence upon an immanent life. As the philosopher of Concord exclaimed: " Here is now a perfect religion, which can be set in an intelligible and convincing manner before all men by their reason."

This is the end of this publication.

Any remaining blank pages are for our book binding requirements and are blank on purpose.

To search thousands of interesting publications like this one, please remember to visit our website at:

Printed in the United States
51160LVS00005B/109